The GIFT

Composed & Illustrated by Darcy Jackson

The Gift
Copyright © 2023 Darcy Jackson (DarcyL)
All rights reserved.
ISBN: 978-1-990871-139

Published by Fictitious Ink Publishing,
Tumbler Ridge, BC, Canada, V0C 2W0

This booklet is devoted to
Lord Jesus Christ and
our Father in heaven.
It is dedicated to
My sisters in Christ;
Amanda and Sheri.
Thank you for your friendship.
I love you both,
DarcyL
❤️

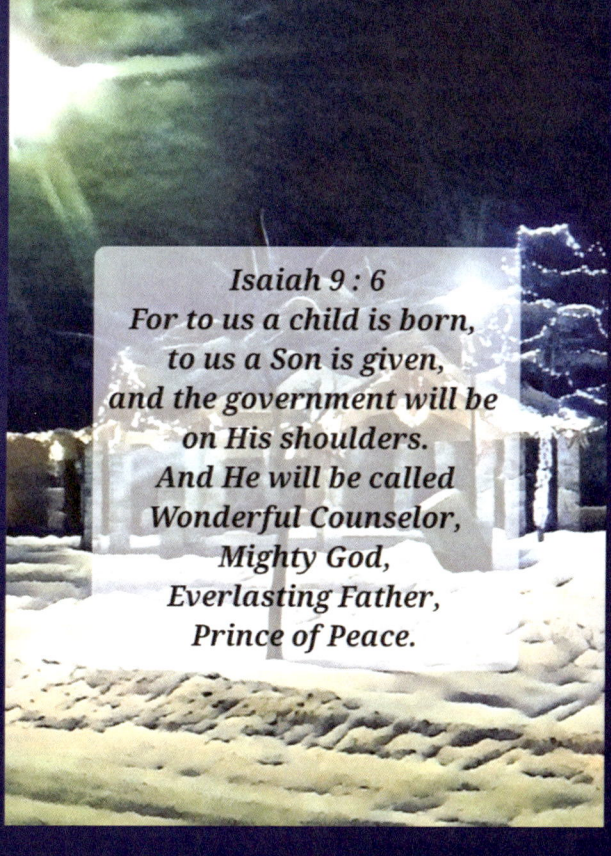

Isaiah 9 : 6
For to us a child is born,
to us a Son is given,
and the government will be
on His shoulders.
And He will be called
Wonderful Counselor,
Mighty God,
Everlasting Father,
Prince of Peace.

ALPHA and OMEGA

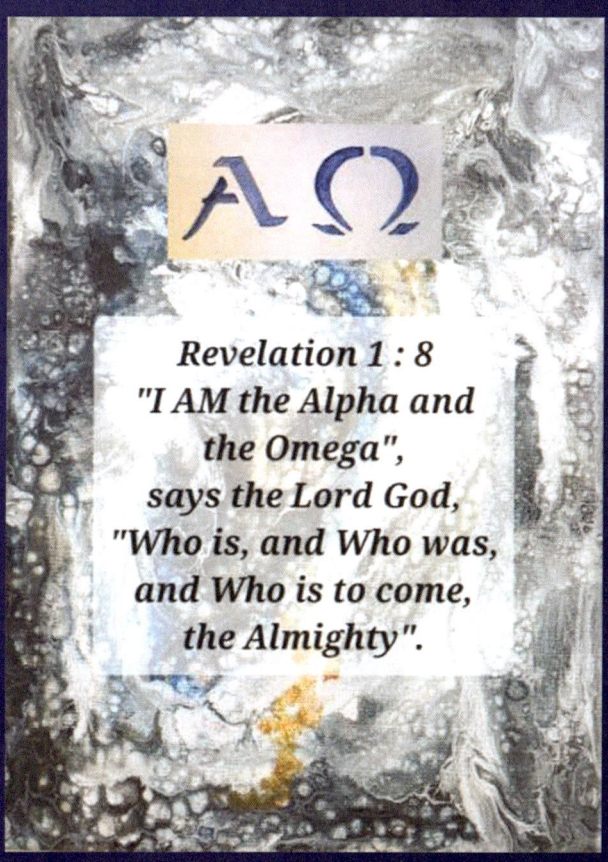

Revelation 1 : 8
"I AM the Alpha and
the Omega",
says the Lord God,
"Who is, and Who was,
and Who is to come,
the Almighty".

BREAD
of LIFE

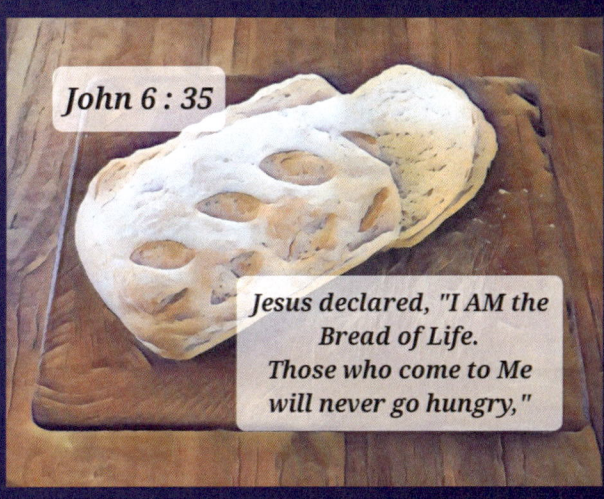

John 6 : 35

Jesus declared, "I AM the
Bread of Life.
Those who come to Me
will never go hungry,"

"and those who believe in Me, will
never be thirsty."

CREATOR

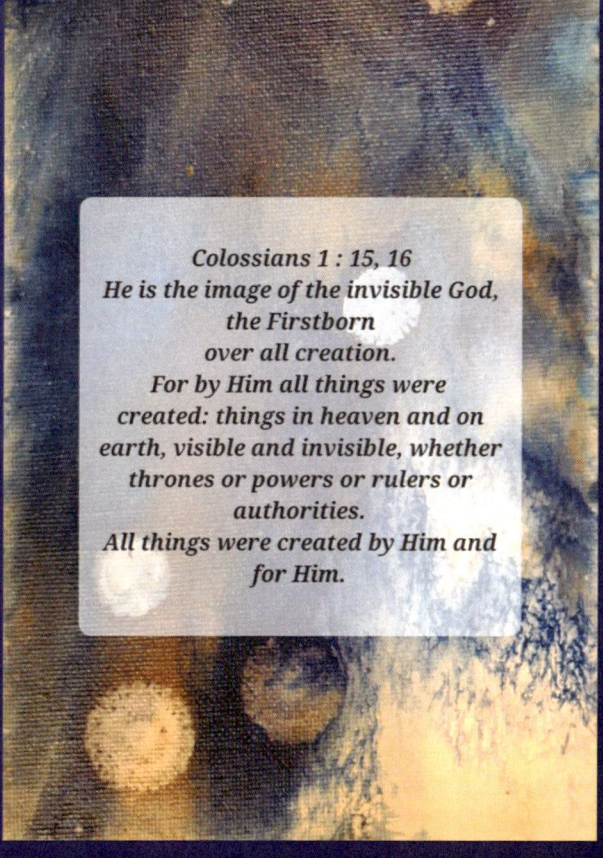

Colossians 1 : 15, 16
He is the image of the invisible God,
the Firstborn
over all creation.
For by Him all things were
created: things in heaven and on
earth, visible and invisible, whether
thrones or powers or rulers or
authorities.
All things were created by Him and
for Him.

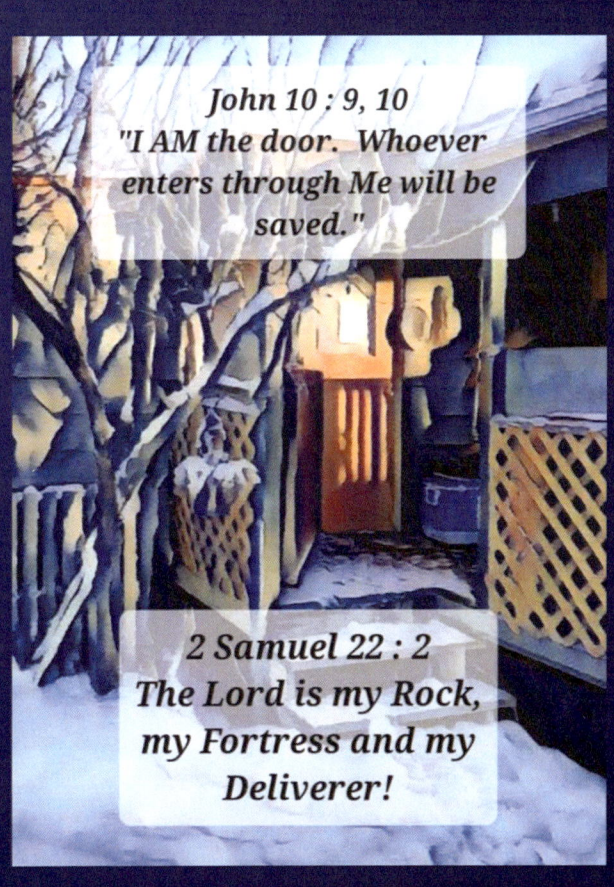

John 10 : 9, 10
"I AM the door. Whoever
enters through Me will be
saved."

2 Samuel 22 : 2
The Lord is my Rock,
my Fortress and my
Deliverer!

**ETERNAL
KING**

Jeremiah 10 : 10
The Lord is the true God.
He is the Living God,
the Eternal King!

1 Timothy 1 : 17
Now to the King Eternal,
immortal, invisible, the
only God - be honor and
glory forever and ever.
Amen

Revelation 1 : 4
Grace and peace to you from
Him Who is, and Who was and
Who is to come,...
and from Jesus Christ, Who is
the Faithful Witness,
the Firstborn from the dead,
and the Ruler of the kings of
the earth.

GOOD
SHEPHERD

John 10 : 11
"I AM the Good Shepherd.
The Good Shepherd lays down His
Life for the sheep."

Worthy Is the Lamb 180

Revelation 5 : 9
They sang a new song: "You
are worthy to take the scroll
and open its seals, because
You were slain, and with
Your Blood, You purchased
people for God from every ,
tribe and language and
people and nation."

HIGH
PRIEST

Hebrews 4 : 14
We have a Great High Priest
who has gone through the
heavens; Jesus the Son of God.
So let us hold firmly to the faith
we profess.

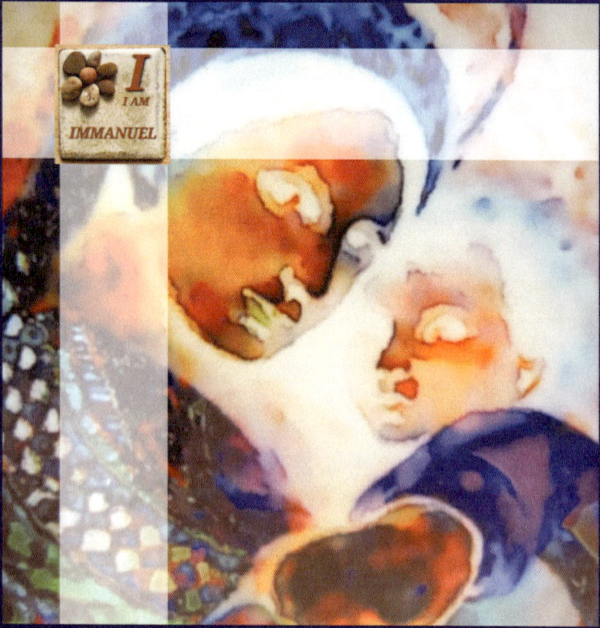

20

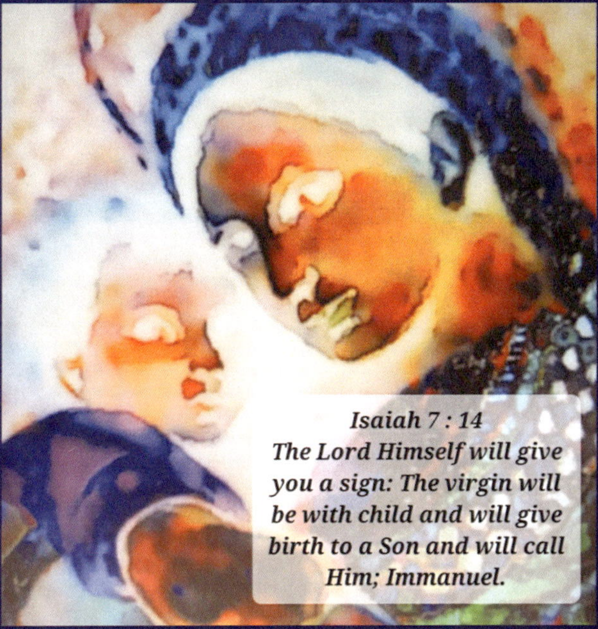

Isaiah 7 : 14
The Lord Himself will give you a sign: The virgin will be with child and will give birth to a Son and will call Him; Immanuel.

IMMANUEL : God with us

J

JESUS

> *Matthew 1 : 21*
> *She will give birth to a Son,*
> *and you are to give Him the name*
> *Jesus, because He will save His*
> *people from their sins.*

JESUS : The LORD saves

KING
of KINGS

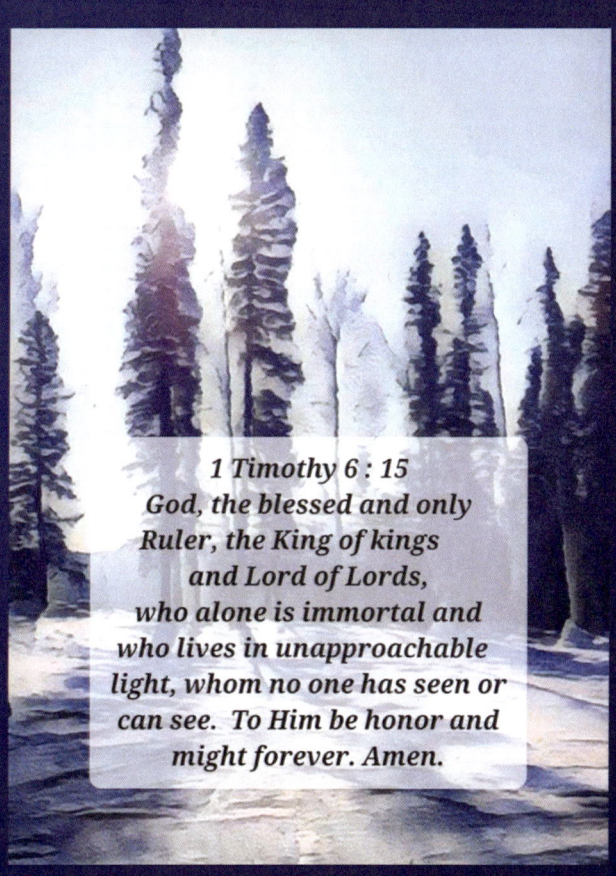

1 Timothy 6 : 15
God, the blessed and only
Ruler, the King of kings
and Lord of Lords,
who alone is immortal and
who lives in unapproachable
light, whom no one has seen or
can see. To Him be honor and
might forever. Amen.

L

LAMB
of GOD

John 1 : 29
The next day, John saw Jesus
coming toward him and said,
"Look, the Lamb of God,
who takes away the sin
of the world!"

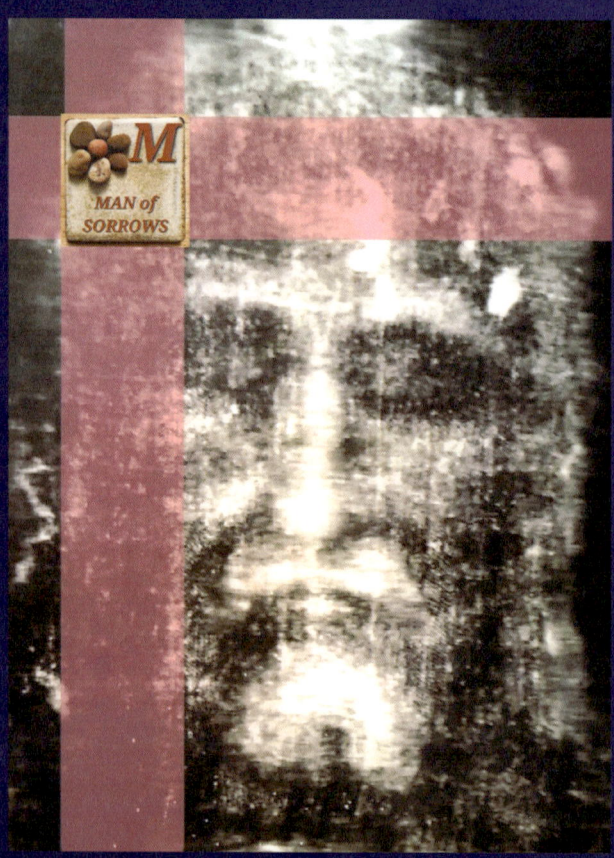

MAN of
SORROWS

28

Isaiah 53 : 3
He was despised and rejected
by men, a Man of Sorrows,
and familiar with suffering.

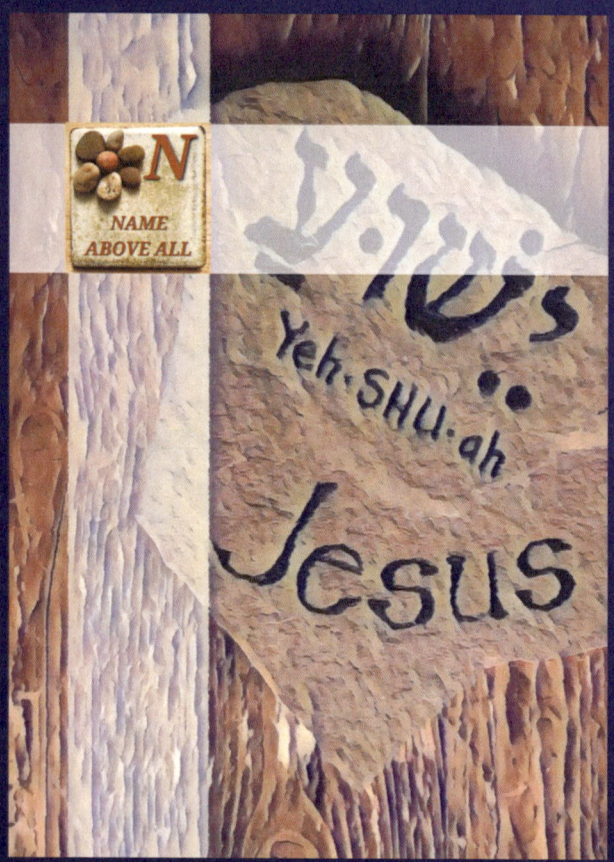

NAME
ABOVE ALL

יְשׁוּעַ

Yeh·SHU·ah

Jesus

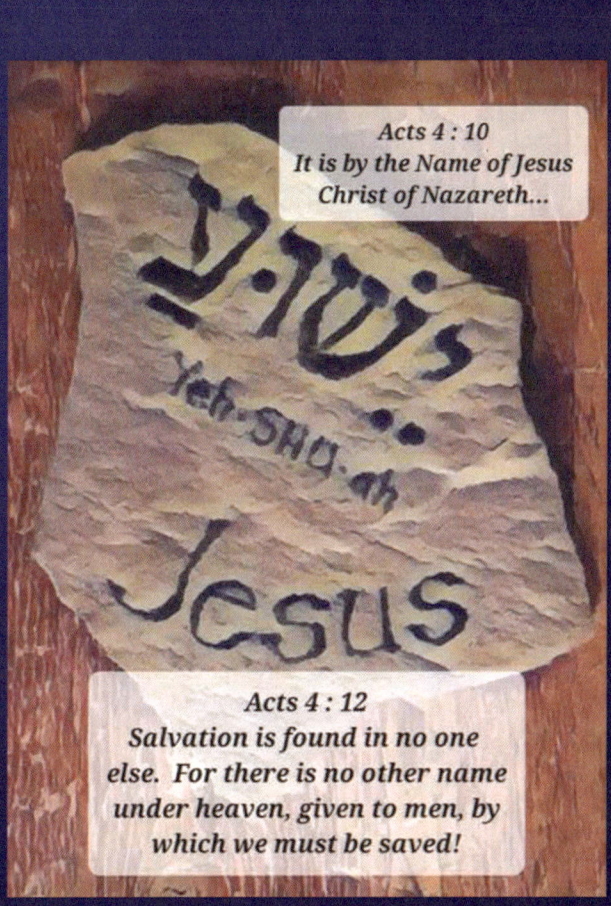

ONLY
BEGOTTEN SON

John 1 : 14
The Word became flesh and
lived for a while among us.
We have seen His glory,
the glory of the Only Begotten
Son,
who came from the Father,
full of grace and truth.

P

PRINCE
of PEACE

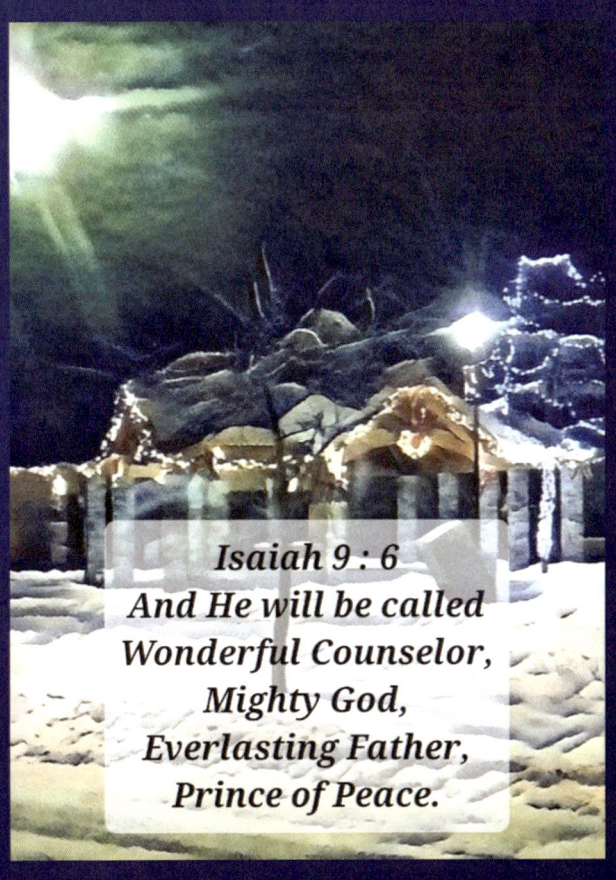

Isaiah 9 : 6
And He will be called
Wonderful Counselor,
Mighty God,
Everlasting Father,
Prince of Peace.

Behold, I come QUICKLY

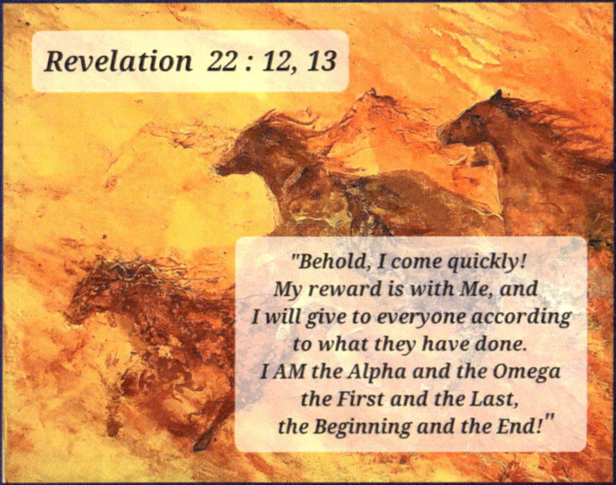

Revelation 22 : 12, 13

"Behold, I come quickly!
My reward is with Me, and
I will give to everyone according
to what they have done.
I AM the Alpha and the Omega
the First and the Last,
the Beginning and the End!"

R ROCK

REDEEMER

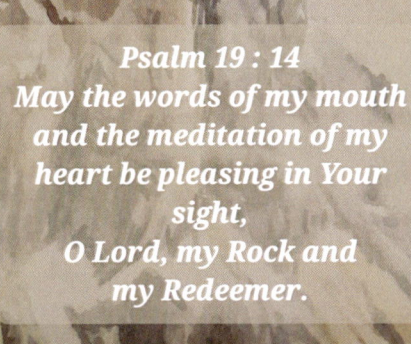

Psalm 19 : 14
May the words of my mouth
and the meditation of my
heart be pleasing in Your
sight,
O Lord, my Rock and
my Redeemer.

S

SAVIOUR

Thankyou Jesus

for being my savior

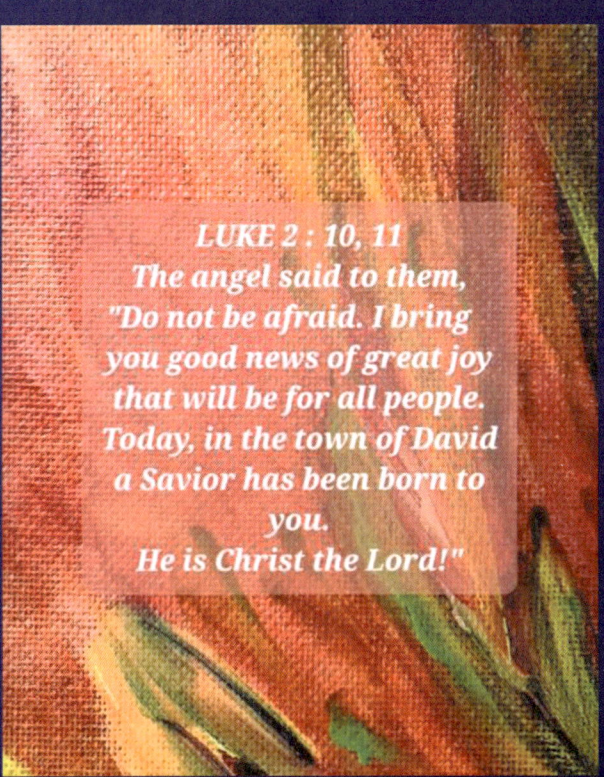

LUKE 2 : 10, 11
The angel said to them,
"Do not be afraid. I bring
you good news of great joy
that will be for all people.
Today, in the town of David
a Savior has been born to
you.
He is Christ the Lord!"

TEACHER

John 13 : 13 - 15

"You call Me 'Teacher' and
'Lord', and rightly so, for that
is what I AM.
Now that I, your Lord and
Teacher, have washed your
feet, you also should wash one
another's feet.
I have set you an example that
you should do as I have done
for you."

UNBLEMISHED
LAMB

Hebrews 9 : 14
How much more will the blood of
Christ,
who through the eternal Spirit,
offered Himself unblemished to God,
cleanse our consciences from
acts that lead to death, so that we
may serve the Living God!

V

VINE

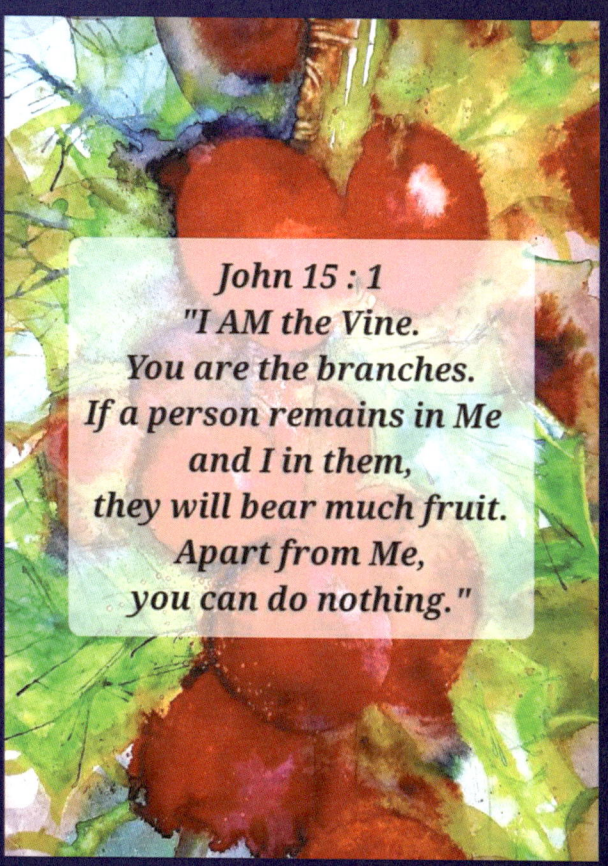

John 15 : 1
"I AM the Vine.
You are the branches.
If a person remains in Me
and I in them,
they will bear much fruit.
Apart from Me,
you can do nothing."

JOHN 17:7

yours; you gave them to me and they have obeyed your word. Now they know that everything you have given me comes from you. ⁸For I gave them the words you gave me and they accepted them. They knew with certainty that I came from you, and they believed that you sent me. ⁹I pray for them. I am not praying for the world, but for those you have given me, for they are yours. ¹⁰All I have is yours, and all you have is mine. And glory has come to me through them. ¹¹I will remain in the world no longer, but they are still in the world, and I am coming to you. Holy Father, protect them by the power of your name—the name you gave me—so that they may be one as we are one. ¹²While I was with them, I protected them and kept them safe by that name you gave me. None has been lost except the one doomed to destruction so that Scripture would be fulfilled.

¹³"I am coming to you now, but I say these things while I am still in the world, so that they may have the full measure of my joy within them. ¹⁴I have given them your word and the world has hated

them, for they are not of the world any more than I am of the world. ¹⁵My prayer is not that you take them out of the world but that you protect them from the evil one. ¹⁶They are not of the world, even as I am not of it. ¹⁷Sanctify⌐ them by the truth; your word is truth. ¹⁸As you sent me into the world, I have sent them into the world. ¹⁹For them I sanctify myself, that they too may be truly sanctified.

Jesus Prays for All Believers

²⁰"My prayer is not for them alone. I pray also for those who will believe in me through their message, ²¹that all of them may be one, Father, just as you are in me and I am in you. May they also be in us so that the world may believe that you have sent me. ²²I have given them the glory that you gave me, that they may be one as we are one: ²³I in them and you in me. May they be brought to complete unity to let the world know that you sent me and have loved them even as you have loved me.

²⁴"Father, I want those you have given me to be with me where I am, and to see my

yours; you gave them to me and they have obeyed your word. 7Now they know that everything you have given me comes from you. 8For I gave them the words you gave me and they accepted them. They knew with certainty that I came from you, and they believed that you sent me. 9I pray for them. I am not praying for the world, but for those you have given me, for they are yours. 10All I have is yours, and all you have is mine. And glory has come to me through them. 11I will remain in the world no longer, but they are still in the world, and I am coming to you. Holy Father, protect them by the power of your name—the name you gave me—so that they may be one as we are one. 12While I was with them, I protected them and kept them safe by that name you gave me. None has been lost except the one doomed to destruction so that Scripture would be fulfilled.

13"I am coming to you now, but I say these things while I am still in the world, so that they may have the full measure of my joy within them. 14I have given them your word and the world has hated

them, for they are not of the world any more than I am of the world. 15My prayer is not that you take them out of the world but that you protect them from the evil one. 16They are not of the world, even as I am not of it. 17Sanctify them by the truth; your word is truth. 18As you sent me into the world, I have sent them into the world. 19For them I sanctify myself, that they too may be truly sanctified.

Jesus Prays for All Believers

20"My prayer is not for them alone. I pray also for those who will believe in me through their message, 21that all of them may be one, Father, just as you are in me and I am in you. May they also be in us so that the world may believe that you have sent me. 22I have given them the glory that you gave me, that they may be one as we are one: 23I in them and you in me. May they be brought to complete unity to let the world know that you sent me and have loved them even as you have loved me.

24"Father, I want those you have given me to be with me where I am, and to see my

John 1 : 1 - 3
In the beginning was the Word, and the Word was with God, and the Word was God. He was with God in the beginning. Through Him all things were made. Without Him nothing was made that has been made.

EXALTED ONE

X

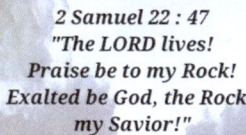

2 Samuel 22 : 47
"The LORD lives!
Praise be to my Rock!
Exalted be God, the Rock,
my Savior!"

Acts 2 : 32, 33
God has raised this Jesus
to life, and we are all witnesses
of the fact.
Exalted to the right hand of God,
He has received from the Father
the promised Holy Spirit
and has poured out what you
now see and hear!

Therefore, let all Isreal be
assured of this: God has
made this Jesus,
whom you crucified,
both Lord and Christ.

YAHWEH

יהוה

Isaiah 42 : 8
I AM the LORD;

יהוה

that is My Name!

Exodus 3 : 15
God also said to Moses,
"Say to the Isrealites:
'The LORD,

יהוה

the God of your fathers
- the God of Abraham,
the God of Isaac and
the God of Jacob -
has sent me to you.'
This is My Name forever

ZION's KING

Psalm 2 : 4
The One enthroned in
heaven,... says:
"I have installed My King
on Zion, My holy hill."

Psalm 9 : 9, 10
The LORD is a refuge for
the oppressed,
a stronghold in times of
trouble.
Those who know Your Name
will trust in You.
For You, LORD, have
never forsaken
those who seek You.

Son of God
JESUS
Son of Man

DIVINITY in HUMANITY

Dear Lord Jesus,
Because of Who You are,
and by what You have accomplished,
"I can love deeply
from a bottomless Source."
Thank You Lord
Thank You Savior
Thank You God
❤️❤️❤️

More in the series!

We hope you found this inspirational
pocketbook uplifting. The simple
affirmative statements, illustrations,
and scriptures were prayerfully compiled
by the author to bring you
strength and peace.

Plus, there are more books in the series!
They'd make a beautiful gift for someone
you love. Available at select bookstores
and online. God bless!

*If you enjoyed this book, please consider
leaving a positive rating or review.*

www.ingramcontent.com/pod-product-compliance
Lightning Source LLC
Chambersburg PA
CBRC090835120626
46547CB00011B/696